Christmas in
the Russian
Renaissance

There is a new mood in Russia today, a renaissance of freedom and openness—as if a door that was locked for more than 70 years had suddenly been opened. Many of the old Communist ways have been tossed aside. New ideas have explod-

of a century—an event that will be remembered for years to come. To the vast majority of the Russian people, this Christmas celebration was a novelty—public celebrations of Christmas had long been forbidden. It is truly astounding to most Russians that Christmas, after its lengthy banishment, is now a legal holiday.

Winter traditions are enjoying a revival in the Russian Renaissance. Here, an appreciative audience watches as an artist sculpts an ice statue in a Moscow park.

ed on the scene, and some old-fashioned values have been restored. Free at last to express themselves, the Russian people have reinstated one of their most cherished celebrations—Christmas.

In 1991, Russia enjoyed its first official Christmas in three-quarters

Clearly, a new revolution is underway in Russia today, and like the revolution of 1917, this one has already had far-reaching consequences, shaking Russian society to its foundations. No one knows where it will end, but one thing is certain—there can be no turning back. Social activity has flowered at all levels of society, with new unions and business associations cropping up daily. The members of the press are now free to criticize the government and present dissenting views. Writers and artists have a new artistic freedom—they can publish stories and display works of art that would have been prohibited only a few years ago. The people are now free to travel to other countries, and religion is once again openly accepted. For these reasons, many people refer to this new era in Russian history as the Russian Renaissance or the Third Revolution.

It is a revolution that has changed the very boundaries of Russia itself. The Soviet Union—once the largest country in the world in area and the third largest in population—was made up of 15 republics. With the demise of Communism, the republics under Soviet control yearned for independence, and have since broken away. Today, the name Russia properly refers to the newly independent nation that was formerly one of the 15 republics that made up the Soviet Union.

These revolutionary changes began in the late 1980's, when Soviet leader Mikhail S. Gorbachev proposed a policy of *glasnost,* or openness. With the advent of glasnost, people were free to express their ideas, and the press could print the truth without fear of government censorship or retribution. Gorbachev also introduced a program of economic reform known as *perestroika.*

When perestroika was introduced, the Soviet economy was in serious trouble. There were severe shortages of food, clothing, and medical supplies. Many basic necessities were difficult to obtain, and empty shelves became a familiar sight in Russia. Perestroika was designed to reverse the damage done during the previous administrations.

Once unleashed, glasnost and perestroika had a snowball effect,

A new revolution is underway in Russia today. Writers and artists have a new artistic freedom — they can publish stories and display works of art that would have been prohibited only a few years ago.

and radical changes soon took place in the political sphere of the Soviet Union, eventually forcing Gorbachev to resign. In June 1991, Boris Yeltsin became the first elected president of the Russian Republic. In September, the activities of the Communist Party were suspended. In December, the Russian Soviet Federative Socialist Republic became the independent nation of Russia, with Yeltsin as its leader.

Two clerks in a toy store do their best to serve a large crowd of customers waiting to buy holiday decorations. Statues of the ever-popular Grandfather Frost and Snow Maiden are among the items on the shelves.

Although many positive results were achieved with glasnost and perestroika, Russia nevertheless remains in a post-revolutionary crisis today. Decades of economic hardship and political oppression cannot be corrected overnight. There are those who fear change and yearn for a return to the old Communist form of government. The move to a free-market economy is a difficult transition period for nearly all the people. Every level of society is affected.

Many people are angry; many others welcome the change. Most are torn between hope and fear.

Glasnost is certainly good news for Christians who want to celebrate Christmas and practice their faith openly. One of the most dramatic changes of the Russian Renaissance has been the government's position on religion.

Not only has the new leadership of Russia given permission for the people to worship without reprisals, it is actively encouraging such behavior. The government hopes that religious ties will strengthen family life and restore old-fashioned values to society, thus holding the country together through a difficult period.

It is estimated that millions of Russians are flocking back to the church, with thousands being baptized every day. Some observers claim that there are as many as 40 million practicing Christians in Russia today, though these numbers are impossible to verify. Without

question, though, there has been an upsurge in religious interest—and in church attendance.

For many Russians, a return to religion represents a return to their old roots and their old culture. Visit an Orthodox church or a Baptist chapel in Russia today and you will be impressed by the size of the congregation. Granted, the majority of the worshipers are older women, but this is changing. A growing number of men and young people are becoming regulars at church services. Those who come every week seem to know

Present-day Russia is a vast region that covers 6,592,849 square miles (17,075,400 square kilometers). The country is bordered on the west and southwest by the other former Soviet republics. Within Russia lies the thinly populated region of Siberia.

53

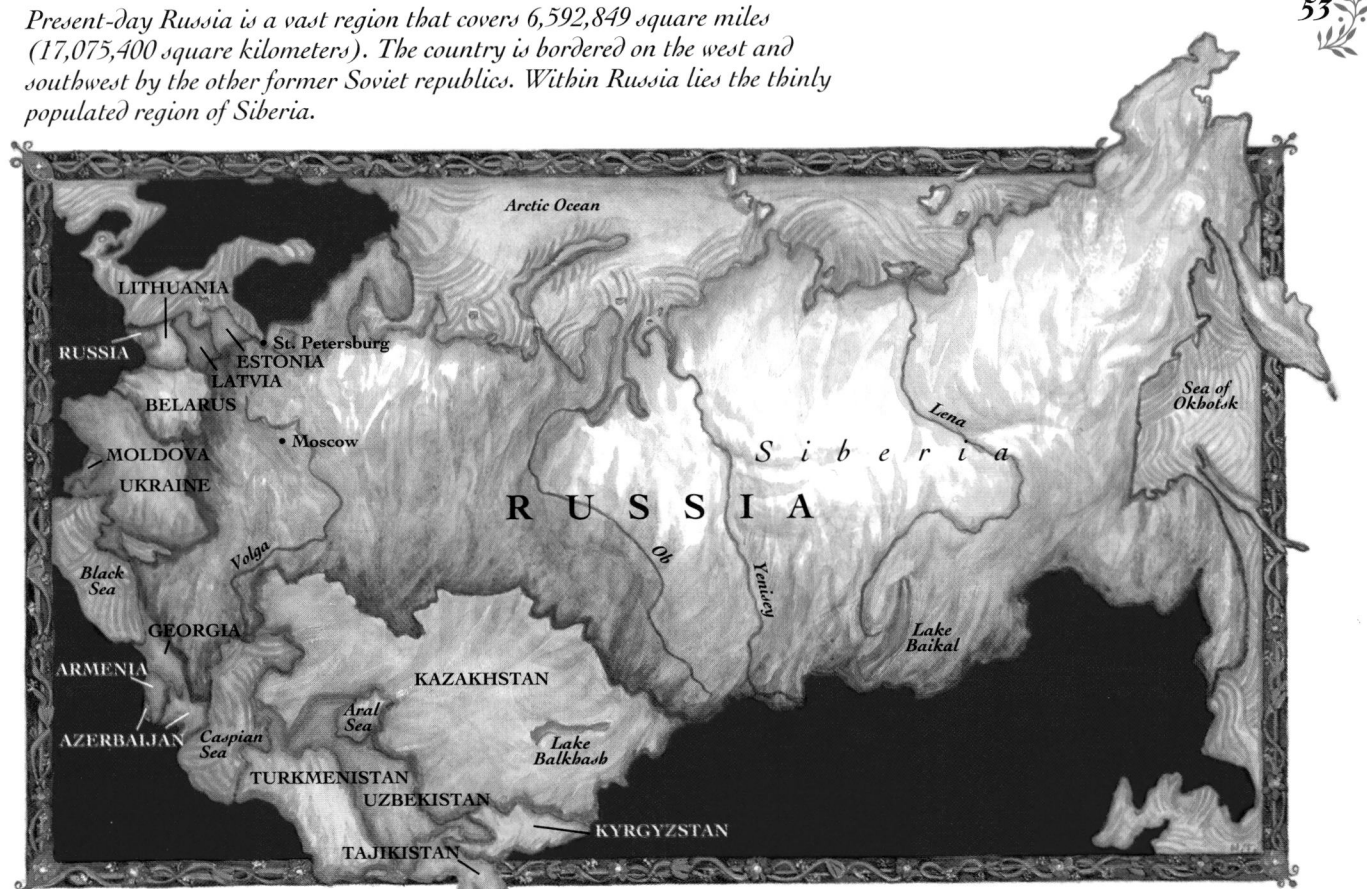

the hymns and prayers by heart, and the intensity of their faith is striking. Many rejoice that they can once again worship openly, without fear. The younger generations have never before experienced religious freedom.

Many churches have reopened throughout Russia, and thousands of new religious societies have registered with the government. Hundreds of church building permits have been issued, allowing new religious structures to be created.

The Russian Orthodox Church, by far the largest religious institution in Russia, is the supreme authority in terms of church teaching. Many of its rituals and services have remained unchanged for hundreds of years. Lately, there has been a resurgence of interest in Orthodoxy, leading to great numbers of conversions.

The Russian Orthodox Church is headed by the patriarch of Moscow and All Russia, who is elected by the Local Council, a group that runs church affairs in conjunction with the Holy Synod. The Russian Orthodox Church currently has more than 8,000 parishes and 74 dioceses.

Many other religious groups also function within Russia's boundaries. The Protestant population includes a significant number of Baptists and Baptist churches. The Roman Catholic Church also has its share of followers, and there are many Muslims. In addition, Russia has more than a million Jews. Whatever the religious preferences of the people, they are now free to practice their faith as they choose.

The congregation swells Moscow's Cathedral of the Epiphany as record numbers of worshipers attend a service on Christmas Eve of 1992.

Russia's winter festivals are also celebrated with a new freedom and enthusiasm now that the renaissance is firmly underway, and some noticeable changes have taken place. On New Year's Day, huge posters of Grand-

Patriarch Alexi II leads a special Christmas service on January 7, 1992 in the Cathedral of the Assumption. The Cathedral is situated on the Kremlin's Cathedral Square, which is also the site of the Cathedral of the Annunciation, Cathedral of the Twelve Apostles, and Cathedral of the Archangel.

father Frost now hang in the Kremlin's halls and museums. As a result, the Kremlin takes on a more festive atmosphere. New Year's once again becomes an occasion for saying good-by to the old year, welcoming the new year, and forgetting one's troubles—and politics—for at least one night.

Just as in previous years, there is a tall New Year's tree in Manezh Square in front of the Kremlin, gaily decorated with multicolored lights and large peasant dolls. Lampposts are decked out with blazing white lights, and electronic billboards flash New Year's greetings. Fireworks shoot boldly into the air from Red Square, illuminating its skyline of medieval towers and graceful onion domes. Thousands gather to drink champagne, sing, and watch the colorful spectacle while they await the stroke of midnight from the chimes of the Spassky Tower. Everyone is bundled up in coats and fur hats. Many young Russians hold sparklers high over their heads. Here and there, groups of people dance in a circle with arms locked and legs kicked up. The sounds of a thousand hoots, whistles, and cheers fill the air. Some wave red roses, while others raise the white, blue, and red flag of Russia.

Russian television stations broadcast the New Year's events in Red Square all over the country. They also broadcast many American-style variety shows. Like their Western

A poster of Grandfather Frost hangs from the entrance to Gorki Park in Moscow. Many public buildings now display Christmas decorations during the holiday season.

counterparts, these specials depict a nation of plenty, with big parties, lots of champagne, extravagant displays of food, and much glitz and fanfare.

As the holiday season is traditionally a time of fortunetelling in Russia, many of the country's more famous psychics and astrologers are asked to give their predictions for the upcoming year. Even though most people do not take this soothsaying seriously, it is great entertainment. The year's most dramatic events are also rehashed and replayed to officially wrap up the old year and usher in the new.

New Year's Eve has always been an extremely popular holiday in Rus-

sia, for both adults and children. In every part of the country, villages and towns spring to life and ring in the new year with fireworks, parties, and champagne. Many people dress up for New Year's Eve and go out on the town with friends. And New Year's is certainly a happy time for the children, who look forward to a visit from Grandfather Frost as they did under the Communist regime, when Grandfather Frost made his rounds on New Year's Eve or New Year's Day. This tradition will probably continue as long as Christmas comes after New Year's in Russia. In any case, most Russian children try to be well behaved—whatever day

Grandfather Frost arrives—to make sure they get their New Year's gifts.

One of the men in a family may dress up as Grandfather Frost for the children. Some families hire an actor to play this role. These performers are often students, and they undoubtedly have as much fun as the children. The arrival of Grandfather Frost is the highlight of the night, if not of the entire year, for most Russian youngsters.

As in previous years, most children open their gifts on New Year's Eve. Others open them on Christmas Eve. Some children are told that Grandfather Frost will come while they're asleep at night, so they had best hasten to bed if they want to find presents in the morning.

New Year's Eve fireworks burst into view behind Spassky Tower in Moscow's Kremlin. A carillon in the tower chimes on the quarter-hour, and on New Year's Eve, an enthusiastic crowd gathers there to "ring in" the new year.

57

A Russian family enjoys a sumptuous dessert on New Year's Eve. The holiday meal can last for hours, ending well after the New Year has been welcomed in.

Some lucky children are among the thousands who participate in the spectacular New Year's Day party at the Kremlin. Here they can watch what must undoubtedly be the "real" Grandfather Frost arriving in a fantasy vehicle that resembles Sputnik or some imaginary contraption. Then comes the Snow Maiden, with her beautiful blonde braids and blue gown, leading a procession of young girls dressed as snowflakes in dazzling white robes and glittering headdresses. After that, a parade of singers, clowns, dancers, and musicians perform for the children.

Unlike American children, Russian children do not seem skeptical if they encounter mulitiple Grandfather Frosts (who may look nothing alike) during the holiday season, such as in shops, at parties, and out on the streets. The children seem to overlook these coincidences in their desire to believe in the magic of the season.

As in the years under Communist rule, games are organized and folk songs sung around the New Year's tree. New Year's is also an excellent excuse to host a feast, and many Russians do so with great enthusiasm. Visitors to Russia often remark that "the shops are always empty, but the tables are full." And this is usually an accurate statement. Despite the recent shortages and hardships, many Russians still manage to obtain the essentials for a holiday feast. Others less fortunate may pool resources with relatives or close friends to create the kind of New Year's feast they enjoyed in previous years. Russians are also noted for their well-stocked pantries, and most people gather supplies for months before the holidays.

Many of the dishes of old Russia are still found on Russian tables today. These include borscht, blini, and, where available, sturgeon, halibut, or herring. Sweets might include baba or kissel. Recently, fresh fruits and vegetables have been even harder to find, but loaves of delicious Russian bread will almost certainly grace many tables. Russians eat bread with almost every meal.

Ever since 1699, when Peter the Great made January 1 the first day of the new year, the Russian people have enjoyed this loud, exuberant holiday. In Russia today, New Year's is still a more important celebration than Christmas—the influence of 70 years of Communism will not be wiped out overnight. But without question, Christmas is making a strong comeback.

In many areas of Russia, the churches are holding their first Christmas services in more than 70 years. Traditionally, the Russian Orthodox Church commemorates two holy days of the year with especially beautiful services—Christmas and Easter.

Christmas services in the Russian Orthodox Church are renowned for their sacred music. The works of many famous Russian composers illuminate the services, including compositions by Dmitrii Bortnianskii, Nikolai Rimsky-Korsakov, and Sergei Rachmaninoff. Some of these works, originally written for church services, are now gaining popularity

59

On January 7, 1992, puppets representing figures from Russian folklore entertained scores of children and parents during the Festival of the Miracle of the Nativity, which took place in Red Square. St. Basil's Cathedral, one of the most recognizable sights in Russia, can be seen in the background.

and can be heard in public concerts as well as in churches.

Most local church choirs spend months selecting and rehearsing the music for the Christmas service, an effort that is greatly appreciated by the congregation, who often join the choir in song. The glamorous old cathedrals, with their onion domes and medieval frescoes, make an ideal setting for the Christmas services. They are always brightened with hundreds of tall, thin candles, hanging garlands, and icons that depict the Nativity. Unlike many churches in the West, however, Russian churches have no other religious scenes or displays.

Perhaps no other country holds services quite like those held in Russia today. While the service is in progress, the priest teaches the vast majority of the congregation the proper responses. It is an unforgettable sight to watch hundreds of people of all ages learn how to make the sign of the cross, genuflect, or receive Communion. Many prayers and hymns are also taught during services. Most of the people seem anxious to learn these rituals and take part in the special services held on

Worshipers fill this church in Moscow on January 6, Russian Christmas Eve. The Russian Renaissance has meant that the people can once again openly attend church services.

Christmas Eve and Christmas Day.

The priests themselves change from their traditional black attire to flowing, ankle-length, white robes embellished with gold embroidery. The patriarch of the Russian Ortho-

Orthodox church broadcasts special services from Moscow. Recently, Patriarch Alexi II of Moscow and All Russia presided over a Christmas Eve service that was broadcast live on Moscow television. He called up-

Cameramen film Patriarch Alexi II, the Patriarch of Moscow and All Russia, leading a service on Christmas Eve. The service took place in Moscow's Cathedral of the Epiphany, also known as the Patriarchal Cathedral.

dox Church and other members of the senior clergy wear a special headdress called a miter at this time.

Christians who can't make it to church can now watch the service on Russian television. Every Christmas Eve (January 6 in Russia), the

on the devout to pray "for the spiritual revival of our people and the recovery of our state."

This represents another dramatic change—one that would have been unthinkable 10 years ago. Now the whole family can gather around the television set and watch religious services in the comfort of their own home, without having to venture out in the cold Russian winter. And those who live far from Moscow can observe these high services as well as any Muscovite. For many Russians, the ability to watch the patriarch of the Russian Orthodox Church lead a service is equivalent to a devout Catholic living in America and watching a Mass broadcast live from the Vatican.

Russian Orthodox priests carry candles, icons, and sacred relics as they process around a Moscow church after a Christmas Eve service.

The year 1991 saw the resurgence of yet another prerevolutionary custom—a religious procession on Christmas Eve known as the *Krestny Khod*. The Krestny Khod is a Christian custom that dates back more than a thousand years and literally means "walking with the cross." It is a procession that takes place around the church after Christmas services are over. In spite of the religious oppression of the last 70 years in Russia, the Krestny Khod was never forgotten. It was always observed on Christmas, wherever churches were open, as well as on certain other religious occasions.

Throughout Russia, after Christmas Eve services, people carrying candles, torches, and homemade lanterns parade around the church, just as their grandparents and great-grandparents did long ago. They proudly bear religious flags and icons. The highest-ranking member of the Russian Orthodox Church traditionally leads the Krestny Khod.

The mood is one of excitement mingled with reverence. The Christmas Eve procession is a colorful, beautiful parade, often taking place under the stars, and most Russians feel privileged to participate in this unique event. The procession eventually completes its circle around the

On Red Square, members of the clergy lead the congregation on a candlelit procession known as the Krestny Khod. St. Basil's Cathedral, shining brightly against the night sky, stands behind them.

local church, and everyone reenters the church. The members of the congregation may sing some religious carols or hymns before going home for a late Christmas Eve dinner.

Today in Russia, many of the traditional Christmas foods of the past have been long forgotten and are no longer served. And by the time Christmas arrives, many people are tired after the New Year's festivities, so the Christmas dinner is quieter. No special foods are prepared.

Everyday dishes, such as salted pickled mushrooms, herring, and various vegetable dishes, are served in abundance. There is usually a lavish display of homemade cookies. The only thing that distinguishes the Christmas dinner from any other meal is a candle set on the table and sometimes wrapped with a garland.

The Christmas dinner is usually eaten in the late afternoon after the family returns from Christmas Day services. The new religious freedom has made Christmas Day a holy day for the entire family once again.

In years past, the Christmas season was a time when the family sang kolyadki. However, no one knows these old songs anymore, except perhaps in the most remote villages. The Bolsheviks made no attempts to suppress the kolyadki—they simply died out on their own. Throughout Europe, many old folk traditions were forgotten during the 1900's as people moved into the modern age. There are several groups of folklore enthusiasts who are now trying to revive the kolyadki, with mixed success. The songs are presented in some areas today by singers and actors in stage performances, and are probably not typical of the impromptu singing of the past. No one knows whether the kolyadki will ever regain popularity in Russia and be sung by the people as they were in days gone by.

Now that Christmas is once again a legal holiday, it may steal some of the thunder from New Year's. Many people predict that the customs traditionally associated with Christmas will revert back to that religious holiday. Russians are already indicating a preference for observing the traditional Christmas customs at Christmas—and not at New Year's. Before too long, the New Year's tree may cease to exist and everyone may have a Christmas tree again. Grandfather Frost may even arrive on Christmas, and not on New Year's. Christmas may once again be the time when gifts are exchanged, and New Year's may have its original traditions of fireworks, parties, and other such festivities. No one knows for sure, but some signs seem to point in that direction. The Russian people of the 1990's seem ready to embrace the ancient and unique customs of a genuine old Russian Christmas.

A Moscow family enjoys a quiet Christmas dinner. After the hubbub of New Year's celebrations, the Christmas meal is a more intimate, subdued occasion.

Russian Crafts

Matrioshka Doll Hanging Ornament

This is a project inspired by the traditional Russian Matrioshka dolls (nesting dolls).

The ornament adopts the idea of "nesting" the different dolls within each other. This ornament adds a twist to the nesting doll idea by making these dolls a hanging ornament—each doll fits into another when the ornament is not hanging. Another twist is that you can personalize your ornament by making a doll for each member of your family, either by drawing the faces of your family members (and even your pet dog or cat) on each doll or by cutting out the faces of family members from photos and pasting them on each doll *(ask your adult partner about this first!)*.

Materials:

compass	crayons, colored pencils,
colored paper	markers, or poster paints
pencil	transparent tape
ruler	scissors
colored yarn	an adult partner
glitter	jingle bell (optional)
colored sequins	photos of family members
	(optional)

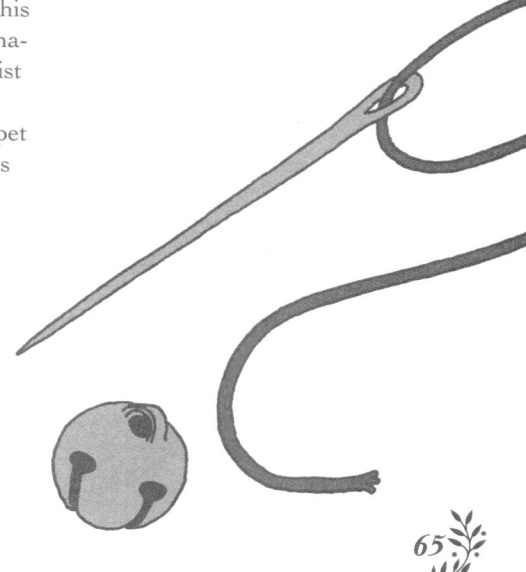

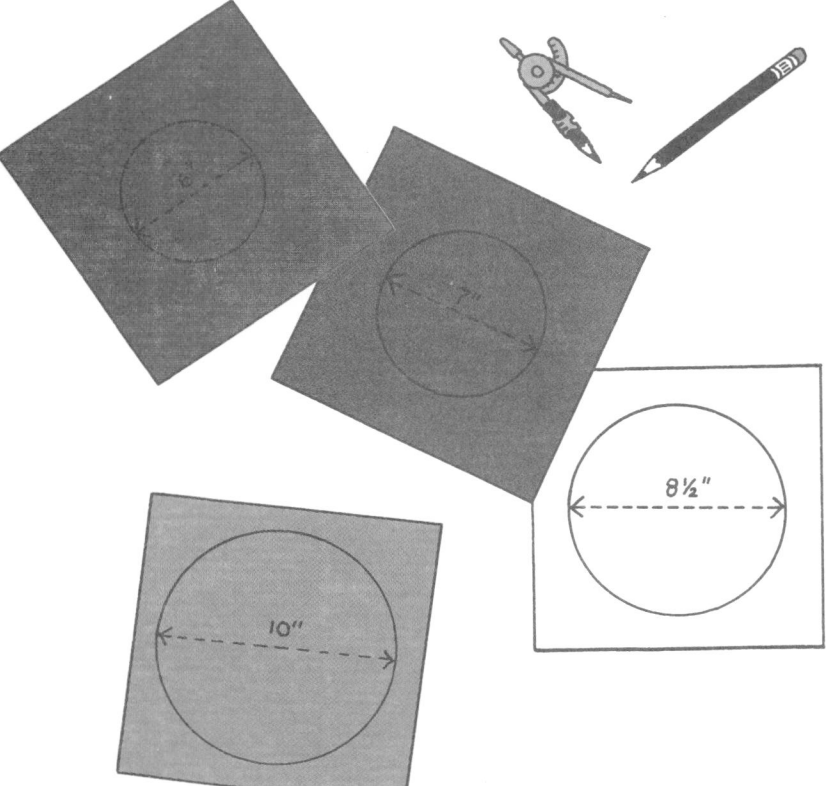

1. Using a compass, draw four circles on four different pieces of colored paper. The first circle should be 10" in diameter, the second one 8-1/2", the third one 7", and the fourth one 6". Next, using a ruler, draw a line to divide each circle in half. Carefully cut out each half-circle. Discard one half-circle of each color, or save them for another project. If you have more than four members in your family, you should start by drawing an amount of circles that matches the number of people in your family. The smallest circle should be no less than 6" in diameter. Cut out as many half-circles as you need, keeping in mind that each half-circle will be made into a cone that should fit into the next largest cone.

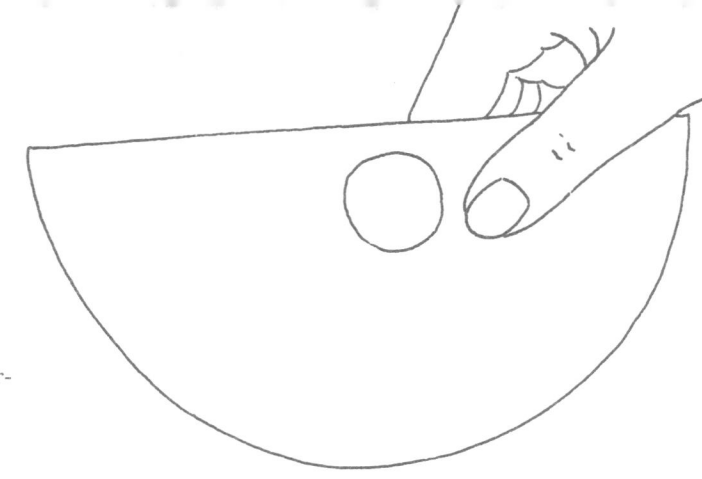

2. Take another piece of colored paper and draw four circles for the dolls' faces. The circles should be 1-1/2", 1-1/4", 1", and 3/4" in diameter for the four dolls previously mentioned. Carefully cut out the small circles and glue them onto the larger half-circles as shown. (Or, if you have been given permission to cut up a few photos, cut out faces of your family members and glue them onto the half-circles.)

3. Draw the faces of your family members on each of the small circles, using crayons, markers, or colored pencils. Don't forget to draw yourself!

4. You can add hair to each doll by drawing it on, or you can use yarn and glue as shown.

5. Give your dolls arms and hands by either drawing them on or cutting them out of colored paper and gluing them on.

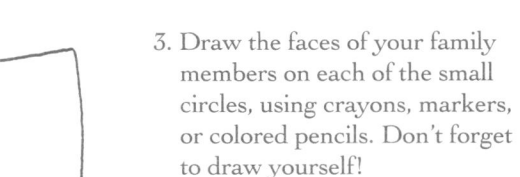

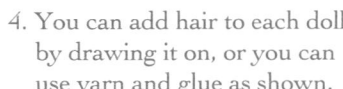

6. Next, create clothes for your dolls. Decorate each doll, using crayons, markers, colored pencils, glitter, sequins, or whatever else you can think of—have fun! (Note: don't put any decorations on the straight-edge area of the cone that will be overlapped when making your cone—see illustration at right.)

7. Now you need to make your doll "cones." Add glue to one half-circle as shown. Overlap the straight ends of the half-circle, press tightly together, and hold in this position until the paper stays together. (See illustration.) Repeat this step with the remaining half-circles.

8. Bend the tip of each cone over to the back of that cone. Secure the tip with a small piece of transparent tape or with a dab of glue under the bend.

9. Ask your adult partner to help you with this next step. Thread the large yarn needle with a piece of colored yarn, about 30" long. Tie a double knot on the long end of the yarn, 4 inches from the end. Working from the inside, take the smallest doll and pierce the bent-over tip of the cone with the threaded yarn needle. Draw the thread through the cone until you reach the knot. (Be careful not to make the hole in the cone too big.)

10. Tie another double knot in the yarn—4-1/4" from the top of the first doll. Pierce the tip of the next-smallest doll and draw the yarn through until you reach the double knot. Repeat this step until you have connected all the dolls.

67

11. When you have finished connecting the dolls, loop the top end of the yarn as shown and knot it close to the tip of the topmost and largest doll.

Now you have your very own hanging Matrioshka doll ornament! If you want, you can tie a jingle bell at the end of the yarn at the bottom of the smallest cone.

Grandfather Frost Tree-Topper

Grandfather Frost is a traditional figure in Russia. Now you can make your own Grandfather Frost decoration to put on the top of your Christmas tree.

Materials:
tracing paper
pencil
repositionable tape
colored paper
white glue
markers, colored pencils, or crayons
cotton balls
gold glitter
gold sticky stars or sequin stars
an empty toilet paper roll cut in half

1. Using tracing paper and a pencil, trace the Grandfather Frost pattern shown in green on this page. Also trace the patterns for the hands, as well as the oval that will be Grandfather Frost's face.

2. Tape the tracing paper to a piece of red or light blue colored paper and cut around the body pattern shape you traced. (Note: do not cut out the oval that will become the face.) Now you have the front of Grandfather Frost. To get the back, take the shape you just cut out and put it down on another piece of red or light blue paper, and trace around the pattern. Then cut out the back piece of Grandfather Frost.

3. Tape the patterns for the face and hands to a piece of pink paper. Carefully cut out the face and two hands.

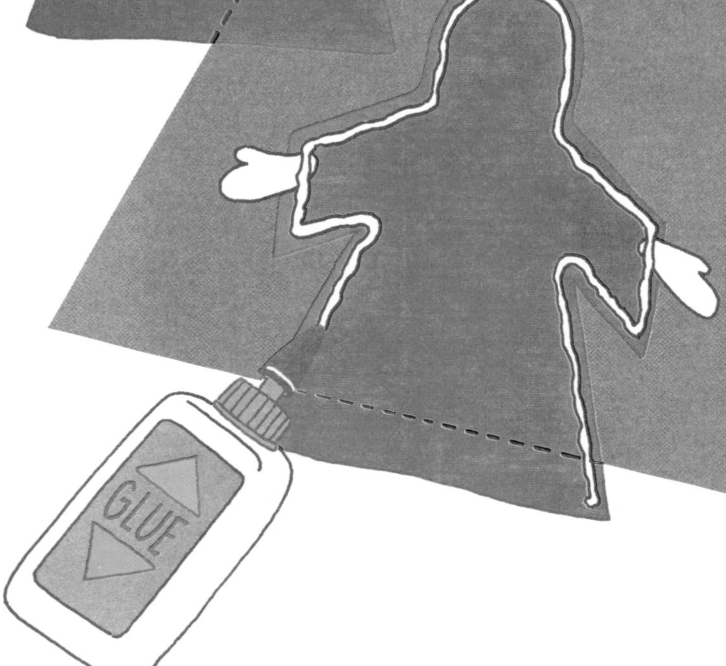

4. Now you are ready to glue your pieces together. First, glue the pink paper oval face onto the front of Grandfather Frost. Next, glue the hands onto the inside of Grandfather Frost's back piece. (See illustration.) Last, put a thin line of glue around the edge of the inside of the back piece of Grandfather Frost, leaving the bottom edge unglued. Press the front piece down onto the back.

5. While the pieces are drying, you can continue decorating the outside of Grandfather Frost. First, draw his eyes, nose, and mouth on the pink oval with markers, colored pencils, or crayons. Next, put a dab of glue on the top of his head and spread it around where his furry hat would be. Take a few cotton balls, pull them apart, and press them down into the wet glue. Now put a dab of glue on the back of Grandfather Frost's head. Use a few more cotton balls, pulled apart, to finish the back of Grandfather Frost's hat.

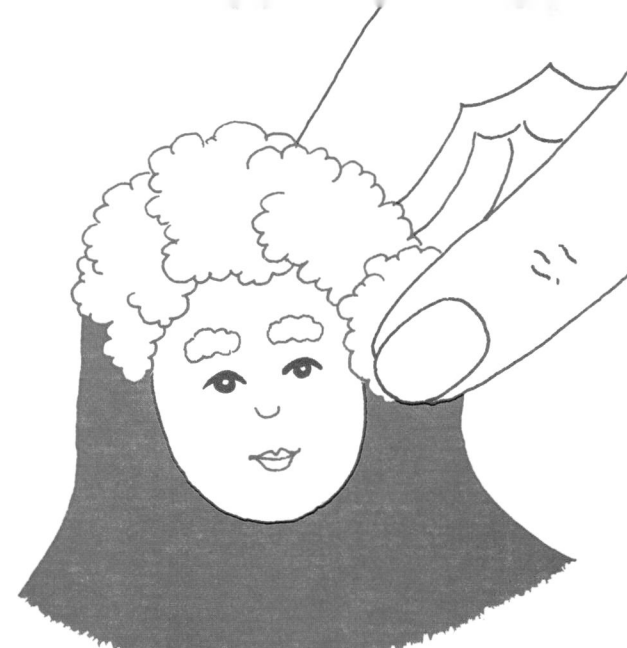

6. Add a little bit of glue to the area around Grandfather Frost's mouth and use more cotton balls to give him a beard and mustache. With a little bit more glue and more cotton balls, you can create furry cuffs on the sleeves and on the front closure and hem of Grandfather Frost's robe.

7. Finish decorating Grandfather Frost's robe using gold glitter and gold stars so that your figure looks like the one shown—or make up your own Grandfather Frost costume!

8. Take an empty toilet paper roll and have an adult help you to cut it in half. Put a little glue on the outside of the tube you cut and spread it all around with your finger. Open up the bottom of Grandfather Frost and stick the tube in until the end is even with the bottom of his robe. Press the front and back of the robe so that they stick to the tube. Hold the tube in position for a minute to set the glue.

69

Now you can put your very own Grandfather Frost at the top of your Christmas tree!

Russian Lacquer Box Gift Wrap

Painting lacquer boxes is a traditional Russian craft that is still practiced today. Each box is made of wood and painted by hand. Some of the boxes have very detailed designs and pictures that tell old folk stories, such as the story of the Snow Maiden. In this project, you will be able to make your Christmas presents look extra special by wrapping them up to look like lacquer boxes—you may even want to make one of these boxes to give as a gift!

Materials:

empty jewelry boxes (or other small- to medium-sized cardboard boxes)	colored paper
	markers, colored pencils, crayons, or poster paint
scissors	old magazines/catalogs
black tissue paper or black wrapping paper	white glue
	colored glitter
	sequins
transparent tape	colored ribbon

70

1. Take an empty box and separately wrap the top and the bottom with the black paper. Be careful that the tape doesn't show too much on the outside of the box pieces.

PAPER SIZE

2. Now you are ready to decorate the lid of the box. Cut a piece of construction paper (any color except black) the same shape as the box top, but make the size a little bit smaller than the actual lid.

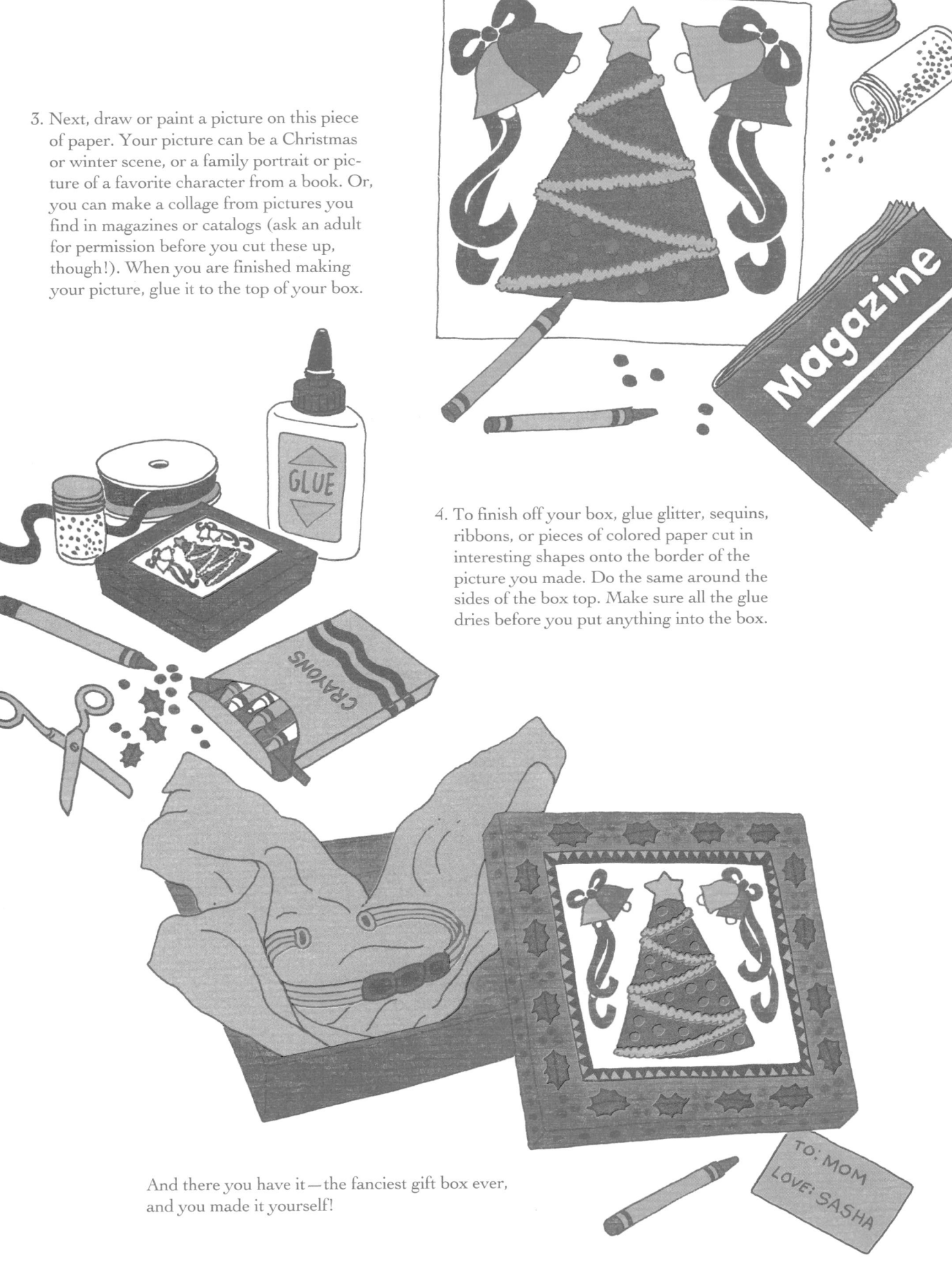

3. Next, draw or paint a picture on this piece of paper. Your picture can be a Christmas or winter scene, or a family portrait or picture of a favorite character from a book. Or, you can make a collage from pictures you find in magazines or catalogs (ask an adult for permission before you cut these up, though!). When you are finished making your picture, glue it to the top of your box.

4. To finish off your box, glue glitter, sequins, ribbons, or pieces of colored paper cut in interesting shapes onto the border of the picture you made. Do the same around the sides of the box top. Make sure all the glue dries before you put anything into the box.

And there you have it—the fanciest gift box ever, and you made it yourself!

Russian Recipes

Kasha Stuffing for Roast Chicken

1 cup coarse kasha (buckwheat groats)
1 egg, slightly beaten
1 tsp. salt
1/8 tsp. freshly ground pepper
8 tbsp. butter
2 to 3 cups boiling water
2 cups onions, finely chopped
1/2 lb. fresh mushrooms, finely chopped

In a medium mixing bowl, toss the kasha and the egg together with a wooden spoon until the grains are well-coated. Transfer to a 12-inch frying pan and cook over moderate heat, stirring constantly, until kasha is lightly toasted and dry; do not allow to burn. Add the salt, 3 tbsp. of the butter, and 2 cups of boiling water. Stir thoroughly, cover the pan tightly, and reduce the heat to low. Simmer for about 20 minutes, stirring occasionally. If at the end of the 20 minutes the kasha seems dried out and is not yet tender, stir in the additional cup of boiling water and cook covered 10 minutes more, or until water is absorbed and buckwheat grains are separate and fluffy. Remove the pan from the heat, remove the cover, and let set for 10 minutes.

While kasha is setting, melt 3 tbsp. of the butter in a 12-inch skillet over high heat. Lower the heat to medium and add the chopped onions. Cook for 2 to 3 minutes, stirring frequently, until the onions are soft and pale gold. Stir the onion into the kasha mixture. Melt the remaining 2 tbsp. of butter in the skillet over high heat. Add the mushrooms to the butter, reduce heat to medium, and cook 2 to 3 minutes, stirring frequently. Then raise the heat to high and cook mushrooms until all the liquid in the pan has evaporated. Stir the mushrooms into the kasha mixture and mix thoroughly. Stuffs one 4- to 5-lb. roasting chicken.

72

White Wine Sauce for Roast Chicken

2 tbsp. butter
1 tbsp. chopped onion or shallots
1 1/2 tbsp. flour
1/2 cup chicken stock
1/2 cup dry white wine
1/2 cup chopped chives
salt

Melt the butter in a saucepan over medium heat. Add the onions or shallots, and sauté until light yellow. Add the flour, stirring until smooth. Gradually add the chicken stock and wine, stirring until sauce is smooth and very hot. Add chives and salt to taste. Makes 1 cup of sauce.

Cabbage Soup (Shchi)

Serves 6 to 8

Stock:
1 lb. lean beef brisket
4 lb. beef marrow bones
1 large onion
1 large carrot
2 celery tops
6 sprigs of fresh parsley
6 sprigs of fresh dill
2 bay leaves

6 peppercorns
1 1/2 tsp. salt

Soup:
4 tbsp. butter
2 cups chopped onions
1 1/2 lb. shredded green cabbage
1 rib of celery, chopped
1 parsley root, scraped and cut
   into fine strips

1 lb. potatoes, peeled and diced
  into 1/4-inch pieces
4 medium tomatoes, peeled, seeded,
  and chopped
1 clove garlic, minced
salt and freshly ground black
  pepper to taste
fresh dill for garnish (optional)

Note: Cabbage soup is best when made a day in advance. You may store it, covered, in the refrigerator, and reheat it slowly when desired.

To make the stock: In a heavy 8-quart pot, bring the brisket, beef bones, and 4 quarts of water to a boil. Skim off any foam as it rises to the surface. Meanwhile, peel and quarter the onion, and peel the carrot. Tie the celery tops, parsley, dill, bay leaves, and peppercorns loosely in a piece of cheesecloth to make a bouquet garni. When the beef and water comes to a boil, add the bouquet garni and salt. Partially cover the pot, and reduce the heat to low. Simmer the mixture until the meat is tender, about 1 1/2 to 2 hours.

To make the soup: While the stock is simmering, prepare the vegetables as follows and set them aside. Shred the green cabbage, and chop the rib of celery. Scrape the parsley root and cut it into fine strips. Peel the potatoes and dice them into 1/4-inch pieces. Peel, seed, and chop the tomatoes. Then melt the butter in a 4-quart pot over moderate heat. Add the onions and cook until they are soft but not brown. Mix in the shredded cabbage, the celery, and the parsley root. Cover the pot, and simmer the mixture over low heat for 15 minutes. Set aside.

When stock is done, strain it through a fine sieve into a large clean bowl. Remove the meat and set aside. Discard the bones and bouquet garni. Using a large spoon, remove and discard as much of the surface fat as possible.

Cut the meat into bite-sized pieces. Add the stock, meat, and garlic to the pot containing the vegetable mixture. Partially cover, and simmer over moderate heat for 20 minutes. Then add potatoes and cook for 20 minutes more. Add the tomatoes and cook for 10 minutes. Add the salt and pepper to taste. Garnish with fresh dill if desired.

Siberian Meat Dumplings (Pelmeni)   Serves 6 to 8

Dough:
3 cups all-purpose flour, sifted
1 teaspoon salt
1 egg, slightly beaten
1 cup cold water

Filling:
2 tbsp. butter
3/4 lb. lean ground beef
1/4 lb. ground pork
1 large onion, minced
2 small cloves garlic, minced
1/4 cup cold water
1/2 tsp. salt
1/4 tsp. freshly ground black pepper

Additional ingredients:
1 egg white, lightly beaten
beef broth (optional)
melted butter (optional)
sour cream (optional)
fresh dill (optional)

In a large bowl, combine the flour and salt. Make a well in the center of the flour, and add the egg and water. Mix thoroughly until the mixture forms a ball. Place the dough on a floured surface and knead until smooth and no longer sticky (about 5 minutes). Cover loosely with a clean linen kitchen towel or wax paper, and set aside in a cool place for 30 minutes to 1 hour.

In a large frying pan, melt the butter. Add the onion and garlic, and sauté until lightly golden. In a large mixing bowl, combine the onions and garlic with the beef, pork, water, salt, and pepper; mix thoroughly. Cover loosely with plastic wrap and set aside.

Divide the reserved dough in half. On a floured surface, roll out half the dough to a thickness of about 1/16 inch; be careful not to tear the dough. Using a cookie cutter or the rim of a small glass, cut out as many 2-inch circles as you can.

Place a small amount of filling (slightly more than 1/2 tsp.) on the lower half of each dough circle. Lightly brush or spread a small amount of the beaten egg white around the edges of each dough circle, and fold over the top to join the edges. Press

the edges together with a fork to seal them. Set aside finished dumplings in a single layer on a plate or baking sheet. Repeat this process with the other half of the dough.

To cook the dumplings, bring 6 quarts of water to a boil in a large pot; add 1 tsp. salt. Drop in half the dumplings and gently boil, stirring occasionally, until the dumplings rise to the surface. This should take about 8 minutes; do not let the dumplings stick together while cooking. (When done, the filling will no longer be pink.)

Remove the dumplings with a slotted spoon and set in a colander to drain well. Repeat this process with the other half of the dumplings.

Dumplings may be served in heated beef broth, or drizzled with melted butter and topped with sour cream and fresh dill.

 74

Kutya

Serves 6

1 cup wheat berries (whole)
4 cups milk, or more as needed
1/2 tsp. salt
1 cup honey
1 cup poppy seeds, ground in a coffee
  bean grinder or food processor
cinnamon

Place the wheat berries in a bowl and add enough water to cover them. Cover the bowl with plastic wrap and soak the wheat berries overnight. Drain them, then simmer them in 4 cups of milk with 1/2 tsp. salt until the wheat berries are tender (about 2 hours). While simmering, check the berries occasionally to make sure there is ample liquid in the pan; if necessary, add more milk.

When the wheat berries are tender, remove them from the heat and drain them. Place berries in a large bowl and set aside.

In a small saucepan, heat the honey over low heat and stir in the ground poppy seeds. Remove from heat.

Stir the honey and poppy seeds into the wheat berries, along with 1/2 to 3/4 cup of boiling water. The mixture should have a slightly soupy consistency. Place mixture in an ovenproof casserole and bake, uncovered, at 325 °F for 20 minutes.

Remove the casserole to a cooling rack, and let stand for 15 minutes. Sprinkle kutya lightly with cinnamon. Serve warm or chilled.

Variations: To this basic kutya recipe, you may add any or all of the following: 1/4 cup chopped dried apricots, 1/4 cup raisins, 1/4 cup toasted slivered almonds. These optional ingredients should be added to the wheat berry mixture just before baking.

Rom Baba

Cake:

1 envelope active dry yeast
6 tbsp. lukewarm water
    (105 °F to 115 °F)
1 tsp. salt
6 tbsp. sugar
6 tbsp. lukewarm milk
    (105 °F to 115 °F)
1/2 cup butter, melted and cooled
    to room temperature
5 eggs, lightly beaten
grated rind of one orange
3 cups all-purpose flour, sifted

Syrup:

1 1/4 cups water
2 1/2 cups sugar
1 1/3 cups rum

Sprinkle the yeast over the water in a large bowl, and stir until yeast is dissolved. Let stand about 5 minutes.

Add the salt, sugar, lukewarm milk, butter, eggs, and grated orange rind and beat with an electric mixer at medium-high speed until batter is smooth (about 4 minutes). Beat at medium speed for about 2 minutes more, adding flour gradually until all flour is thoroughly mixed in. Batter should be smooth and shiny.

Cover the bowl with a damp linen kitchen towel and let rise in a warm, draft-free place until batter has doubled in volume, about 1 hour.

Generously grease a 1 1/2-quart ring mold or bundt pan. Beat the risen dough for 2 minutes, then transfer it to the mold or bundt pan; it should fill the mold or pan halfway. Let the batter rise, uncovered, in a warm, draft-free place until it has doubled in volume, about 30 to 35 minutes. Batter should now reach the top of the mold or pan.

Preheat the oven to 425 °F. Bake the cake for 25 to 30 minutes, or until a cake tester comes out clean.

Run a knife around the edge of the mold or pan. Invert cake on a rack and let cool for at least 15 minutes.

While cake is cooling, prepare the syrup. In a small saucepan, combine the water and sugar. Simmer until the sugar is completely dissolved, about 10 minutes. Remove the pan from the heat; allow to cool slightly, then stir in the rum.

Place the cooled cake on a plate. Poke holes all over the cake with a skewer, then pour the syrup evenly all over the cake. Let stand; use a large spoon to baste the cake every 10 minutes with the syrup that collects on the plate. Repeat process until almost all the syrup is absorbed. Serve cake with whipped cream or vanilla ice cream.

75

Russian Carols

Let Us Praise Thee

English Lyric by Olga Paul

Arranged by Felix Guenther

Kaleahdah Maleahdah

"Christmas Missmas"

N. Rimsky-Korsakov

Oh! Across the river there burns a fire,

On the bench a girl is sitting. Ka - le - ah - dah, ma - le - a - dah!

Kolyada, Kolyada

Father Christmas or Santa Claus

English Version by Cecil Cowdrey

Anonymous

1. Ko - ly - a - da, — Ko - ly - a - da, Walks a-bout on Christ-mas eve.
2. Ko - ly - a - da, — Ko - ly - a - da, Come this Ho-ly Night, we pray.

1. Ko - ly - a - da, — Ko - ly - a - da, At the win - dow, cakes to leave.
2. Ko - ly - a - da, — Ko - ly - a - da, Came and brought us Christ-mas Day.

lossary

baba (bä′bə), a small, spongy, light cake, made with yeast.

balalaika (bal′ə lī′kə), a Russian musical instrument somewhat like a guitar, with a triangular body and usually with three strings.

blini (blin′ē), a very light, thin, small pancake, served with sour cream, or caviar, smoked salmon, or other delicacy.

Bogoroditsa (bəgər o′ditsä), a Russian name for the mother of Christ.

borscht (bôrsht), a Russian soup consisting of meat stock, cabbage, beets, and potatoes, served with sour cream.

boyar (bo yar *or* boi′ər), a member of a former high-ranking order of the Russian aristocracy.

D'yed Moroz (ded′ mə roz′), Grandfather Frost, a legendary Russian gift-giving figure who appears during the holiday season.

gadanie (gədä′ nēe), guessing games, often played in old Russia during the Christmas season in an attempt to foretell the future.

glasnost (gläs nôst′), a policy of open and public discussion of domestic issues encouraged by the former Soviet government.

gusla (güs′lə), a Russian stringed musical instrument played by plucking.

karavay (kərəväi), a round bread made from rye or wheat, with designs on the top in the shape of animals, flowers, or other subjects.

kasha (kä′shə), coarse grains of buckwheat, barley, wheat, or millet.

kissel (kēsel′), a berry custard made with cranberries, strawberries, or raspberries.

kolyadki (kəlyäd′ kē), Russian carols sung during the Christmas season in old Russia.

krestny khod (krest′ nyi khôd), a religious procession that takes place on Christmas Eve.

kutya (kōōtyä′), a rich, sweet porridge made of wheat berries, poppy seeds, and honey.

matrioshka (mətryôsh′ kə), a particular kind of set of dolls, in which the dolls are graduated in size and "nest" inside each other.

78

Novyi God (nô´vyi god´), the Russian name for the New Year's holiday.

otstoyat (ətstəyät´), literally, "to stand the service"; the Russian phrase for attending a church service.

pelmeni (pēlme´ nē), miniature dumplings filled with beef and pork.

perestroika (per´ə stroi´kə), a major reform of Soviet society, especially in economic policy, during the 1980's.

piroshki (pirəshkēē), small turnovers stuffed with meat, fish, chicken, or egg and vegetables.

podbliudnye (pədblyōōd´ nye), Russian prophetic songs formerly sung during the Christmas season.

rom-baba (rôm´ bä´bə), a small, spongy, light cake, made with yeast and flavored with rum.

S Novym Godom (ss-nô´vem gô´dəm), the Russian words for "Happy New Year."

S Rozhdestvom Khristovym (ss-rəzhdestvôm khrēstô´vym), the Russian words for "Merry Christmas."

shchi (shchee´), a Russian cabbage soup, often made with meat, fish, grains, or vegetables.

Snegurochka (snigōō´rəchkə), the Snow Maiden; a legendary Russian figure sometimes said to be the granddaughter of Grandfather Frost.

Soyuz Sovetskikh Sotsialisticheskikh Respublik (səyōōz´ səvets´kēkh sətsēəlē stē´chə skikh respōōb´lēk), the Russian phrase for "Union of Soviet Socialist Republics."

Sviatki (svyät´kē), the Christmas season in Russia; in old Russia, it lasted from December 25 to January 7. In present-day Russia, it lasts from January 7 to January 19.

troika (troi´kə), a Russian sleigh pulled by three horses harnessed abreast.

zakuski (zä küs´ kē), hors d'oeuvres; appetizers.

79

cknowledgments

Cover: © Uniphoto, artwork by Natalia G. Toreeva

1: World Book photo by Joann Seastrom
2: Novosti from Gamma/Liaison
6-8: Sovfoto
10-11: The Great Encyclopedia of Russia Publishing House
12: V. Solomatina
13: The Great Encyclopedia of Russia Publishing House
16: R. Koutcherov/The Great Encyclopedia of Russia Publishing House
18-22: The Great Encyclopedia of Russia Publishing House
24-26: Natalia G. Toreeva
28-30: *27 February, 1917* by Boris Kustodiev/The Great Encyclopedia of Russia Publishing House
32: The Great Encyclopedia of Russia Publishing House
33: U. Rakootin
34-36: The Great Encyclopedia of Russia Publishing House
37: Novosti from Gamma/Liaison
38: Tass from Sovfoto
39: World Book photo by Joann Seastrom
40: © Andy Hernandez, Sipa Press
42-43: The Great Encyclopedia of Russia Publishing House
44: Tass from Sovfoto
47: Natalia G. Toreeva
48-50: Novosti from Sovfoto
52: © Patrick Robert, Sygma
53: Natalia G. Toreeva
54: © East News from Sipa Press
55: The Great Encyclopedia of Russia Publishing House
56: © Gary Henoch, Gamma/Liaison
57: G. Galazka, Sipa Press
58-59: © East News from Sipa Press
60: Novosti from Sovfoto
61-62: © Chip Hires, Gamma/Liaison
63: © East News from Sipa Press
64: The Great Encyclopedia of Russia Publishing House
65-71: Eileen Mueller Neill

Advent calendar: artwork by Mariana Beliayeva
Recipe cards: World Book photos by Dale DeBolt